MW00978090

Best Instant Pot Stew and Soup Cookbook

Healthy and Easy Soup and Stew Recipes for Pressure Cooker

By

Helena Walker

Copyright [Helena Walker]

TABLE OF CONTENTS

INTRODUCTION

No matter the time of year, nothing can be more satisfying than a hot bowl of soup. Much of the appeal of this comfort food comes from its delightful aromas and so many different flavors and styles, whether clear, creamy or thick with vegetables. But more than ever stew and soups are a way to bring seasonal flavors to the table. Soup is versatile, serving as everything from a first course to lunch to a hearty standalone meal and even breakfast.

Why is soup good for health? Soup is nutritious because of the variety of ingredient combinations; you can combine vegetables, herbs, spices, grains, and meat. It can be a full meal, a healthy side dish, or a snack. Not only is it easy to prepare and tasty, but it can also be economical as well. Soup can be filling and satisfying, making it ideal for weight management. Soup is the combination of carbohydrates, proteins, and other nutrients, as well as being easy to digest, it gives a steady supply of energy to our bodies. The ample nourishment and the boost of energy with soup make it the perfect healthy food.

Vegetable soup contains many vitamins, such as vitamin A, C, D, and the mineral calcium. One health study proved that tomato soup is the best source of antioxidants and lycopene that may help to reduce the risk of cancer. Soups made up of meat, beans and fish contain lean protein whereas beans are rich in fiber. The healthiest soup includes fresh vegetables, low-fat ingredients and a minimum amount of salt.

This book contains various types of delicious instant pot soup & stew recipes. Instant pot is one of the electric pressure cooker appliances. It is also called a multi-cooker that can do the job of the pressure cooker, rice cooker, slow cooker, steamer and more. Instant Pot is a new way of cooking a healthy and delicious meal at home. This book contains 50 healthy and delicious soup & stew recipes.

Soup & Stew Health Benefits

- Nutrient Rich: Soup is nutrient rich because it is made up of a variety of ingredients such as fresh vegetables, meat, spices, herbs, grains, and fruits.

- Energy booster: Soup contains proteins, carbohydrates, and various nutrients; it provides steady energy to our body.

- Easy to prepare and economical: Soup is very easy to prepare and also economical, it requires some fresh vegetables and less amount of other ingredients.

- Aids weight loss: Soup is low in calories and rich in nutrients it helps to reduce or maintain body weight.

- Rich in fibers: some vegetable soup and legumes soup are high in fibers, it helps to keep your digestive system healthy and prevents bloating.

INSTANT POT FUNCTIONS

- **Manual:** This function is used to adjust manual pressure, temperature and time setting selecting the + / - buttons.

- **Sauté:** This function is used to sauté your food. When using sauté mode instant pot lid must be open and you can adjust the temperature using the less, normal, and more settings. You just need to add some cooking oil into an inner pot and add your food and cook.

- **Keep Warm/Cancel:** This function is used to cancel any running program and after pressing this button your instant pot stops the current running program and goes to standby mode. Keep warm function is automatically started when your instant pot goes on standby mode.

- **Steam:** This function is used for steaming vegetables and seafood. When you steam any food make sure steam rack is inserted in the pot otherwise food may burn and stick to the bottom of the pot.

- **Meat /Stew:** Using this function you can make meat/stew dish in the instant pot. You can adjust the settings depending on the texture you want. The default setting of this function is high pressure at 35 minutes. You can adjust it manually also in between 20 to 45 minutes high pressure.

- **Slow Cook:** This function converts your instant pot into slow cooker. When using slow cook function always remember that pressure valve set to the venting position. It allows steam to escape when your dish cooks. This function has 4 hours of default cook time. You can use the + / - buttons to adjust cooking time.

- **Poultry:** This function is used to cook your chicken recipes. The default setting is at high pressure for 15 minutes. You can also adjust the 5 to 30 minutes at high pressure.

- **Soup:** This function is used to cook different types of broth and soups. The instant pot controls temperature and pressure inside so liquid doesn't boil.

- **Rice:** This function is used for cooking rice in the instant pot. Using this function, you can cook your rice in half the time compared to a rice cooker. It takes 4 to 8 minutes to cook rice.

- **Porridge:** This function is used to prepare oatmeal and porridge. Default to high pressure for 20 minutes.

INSTANT POT BENEFITS

There are various types of benefits of the instant pot which are as follows:

- **Safe to use:** Instant pot comes with 10 built-in safety technology features, so using an instant pot makes it super safe to use. Due to the safety mechanisms, it is very safe appliance to use. Its temperature and pressure sensing technology helps to regulate inside temperature and inside pressure.

- **Preserves Vitamins and Nutrients:** Many of the vitamins and nutrients are water soluble at the time of cooking these vitamins and minerals are dissolved in water. While the instant pot requires less water to cook food compared to another cooking method, due to this vitamins and minerals are prevented from dissolving into water. When you are pressure cooking food, the heat, pressure, and steam are even, quickly distributed into the instant pot.

- **Saves Time and Energy:** Instant pots cook food at high pressure which will help to save your cooking time. It cooks food faster than compared to any other traditional cooking method. It saves up to 70% of energy compared to any other cooking methods. The inner pot is fully insulated in an instant pot, due to this it consumes less energy to heat up. It will boil faster because it requires less liquid.

- **Single Pot Cooking:** Instant Pot is also known as a multi-cooker. You can cook various dishes in different styles in a single pot. Instant pots offer you versatile cooking options like you can make breakfast recipes, porridge, oatmeal, yogurt etc. You can make noodles and risottos. You can also make stew, soups, cake etc.

- **Kills Harmful Microorganisms:** Instant pots cook food under high pressure they create a higher temperature 100-degree centigrade which is higher than the boiling point of water. The result of this is that all harmful microorganisms such as viruses, fungi, and bacteria are killed under high-pressure of cooking.

- **Easy to use:** Instant pots come with various pre-programmed functions. You can use predefined functions, or you can manually adjust the cook time, temperature and pressure of the instant pot.

POULTRY SOUP & STEW

1-Perfect Chicken Noodle Soup

Preparation Time: 10 minutes

Cooking Time: 30 minutes

Serve: 4

Ingredients:

- 2 chicken breasts, boneless
- 1 cup egg noodles
- ½ tsp ground ginger
- 8 cups chicken stock
- 1 bay leaf
- ½ tsp dried thyme
- 4 peppercorns
- 3 garlic cloves, minced
- 2 carrots, diced
- 1 onion, diced
- 2 tbsp olive oil

- Pepper
- Salt

Directions:

- Add olive oil in the instant pot and set the pot on sauté mode.
- Add garlic, onion, and carrots to the instant pot and sauté for 3-4 minutes.
- Add remaining ingredients except noodles to the pot and stir well.
- Seal pot with lid and cook on manual high pressure for 10 minutes.
- Release pressure using the quick release method then open the lid.
- Remove chicken from pot using metal tongs.
- Shred the chicken using a fork and set aside.
- Set instant pot on sauté mode. Add egg noodles and cook for 10 minutes or until noodles are soft.
- Return shredded chicken to the pot and stir well.
- Serve and enjoy.

Nutritional Value (Amount per Serving):

- Calories 302
- Fat 14.4 g
- Carbohydrates 18.2 g
- Sugar 4.3 g
- Protein 25 g
- Cholesterol 77 mg

2-Delicious Chicken Orzo Soup

Preparation Time: 10 minutes

Cooking Time: 7 minutes

Serve: 6

Ingredients:

- 2 chicken thighs, skinless, boneless and cut into chunks
- 2 cups fresh baby spinach
- 2 tbsp fresh lemon juice
- ½ cup orzo pasta, uncooked
- ½ tsp lemon zest
- 5 cups chicken stock
- 1 tsp fresh rosemary, chopped
- 2 garlic cloves, minced
- 1 cup carrots, chopped
- 1 celery stalk, chopped
- 1 onion, chopped
- 2 tbsp olive oil
- ¼ tsp black pepper
- ¼ tsp salt

Directions:

- Add olive oil into the instant pot and set the pot on sauté mode.

- Add onion to the pot and sauté until onion is softened about 3 minutes.
- Add garlic, carrots, and celery and sauté for a minute.
- Add chicken, pepper, rosemary, and salt and stir well.
- Add stock, pasta, and lemon zest and stir well.
- Seal pot with lid and cook on manual high pressure for 3 minutes.
- Release pressure using the quick release method than open the lid.
- Add spinach and lemon juice and stir well.
- Serve and enjoy.

Nutritional Value (Amount per Serving):

- Calories 263
- Fat 9.3 g
- Carbohydrates 26.3 g
- Sugar 2.9 g
- Protein 18.8 g
- Cholesterol 43 mg

3-Creamy Salsa Chicken Soup

Preparation Time: 10 minutes

Cooking Time: 30 minutes

Serve: 6

Ingredients:

- 1 lb chicken breasts, skinless, boneless, and cut into chunks
- 2 tbsp fresh parsley, chopped
- 3 tsp taco seasoning
- 1 ½ cups salsa
- 8 oz cream cheese, softened
- 3 cups chicken stock

Directions:

- Add stock, taco seasoning, and salsa to the instant pot and stir well.
- Add chicken to the pot.
- Seal pot with lid and cook on high pressure for 25 minutes.
- Release pressure using the quick release method than open the lid carefully.
- Transfer chicken to a plate.

- In a bowl, add cream cheese and 1 cup hot water and mix well and pour into the instant pot. Stir well.
- Set pot on sauté mode. Shred the chicken using a fork.
- Return shredded chicken to the pot and cook soup on sauté mode for 3-5 minutes.
- Garnish with parsley and serve.

Nutritional Value (Amount per Serving):

- Calories 300
- Fat 19.2 g
- Carbohydrates 5.9 g
- Sugar 2.5 g
- Protein 26.1 g
- Cholesterol 109 mg

4-Chicken Broccoli Soup

Preparation Time: 10 minutes

Cooking Time: 20 minutes

Serve: 8

Ingredients:

- 1 lb chicken breasts, boneless
- 2 ½ cups broccoli, chopped
- 1 cup of water
- 10 oz cream of chicken soup
- 3 garlic cloves, minced
- 2 tbsp butter
- ¼ tsp paprika
- ¼ tsp black pepper
- Salt

Directions:

- Season chicken with paprika, pepper, and salt and set aside.
- Add butter into the instant pot and set the pot on sauté mode.
- Add chicken to the pot and cook until lightly browned from both the side.
- Transfer chicken to a plate.

- Add garlic to the pot and sauté for minutes.
- Add water and chicken soup and stir well.
- Return chicken to the pot along with broccoli.
- Seal pot with lid and cook on high pressure for 10 minutes.
- Release pressure using the quick release method rather than open the lid.
- Remove chicken from pot and shred using a fork.
- Return shredded chicken to the pot and stir well.
- Serve and enjoy.

Nutritional Value (Amount per Serving):

- Calories 177
- Fat 9.2 g
- Carbohydrates 4.9 g
- Sugar 0.7 g
- Protein 18.2 g
- Cholesterol 61 mg

5-Hearty Curried Chicken Soup

Preparation Time: 10 minutes

Cooking Time: 20 minutes

Serve: 6

Ingredients:

- 2 lbs chicken thighs, skinless, boneless, and cut into chunks
- ¼ cup fresh parsley, chopped
- 1 cup of coconut milk
- 2 ½ cup spinach, chopped
- 1 cup tomatoes, chopped
- 4 cups chicken stock
- 1 ½ tbsp curry powder
- 1 tbsp ginger paste
- 2 tbsp garlic, minced
- 1 large onion, chopped
- 2 tbsp butter
- ¼ tsp black pepper
- Salt

Directions:

- Add butter into the instant pot and set the pot on sauté mode.
- Add onion to the pot and sauté for 2 minutes.
- Add ginger paste and garlic and sauté for a minute.
- Add curry powder, pepper, and salt and stir well.
- Add chicken and stir to coat with spices.
- Add tomatoes and stock and stir well.
- Seal pot with lid and cook on manual high pressure for 5 minutes.
- Allow to release pressure naturally for 10 minutes then release using the quick release method. Open the lid carefully.
- Set pot on sauté mode. Stir in coconut milk and spinach and cook on sauté mode until spinach has wilted.
- Garnish with parsley and serve.

Nutritional Value (Amount per Serving):

- Calories 452
- Fat 25.4 g
- Carbohydrates 9.4 g
- Sugar 3.8 g
- Protein 46.6 g
- Cholesterol 145 mg

Helena Walker

6-Tasty Chicken Stew

Preparation Time: 10 minutes

Cooking Time: 18 minutes

Serve: 4

Ingredients:

- 2 chicken breasts, skinless and boneless
- ½ cup of frozen green beans
- 1 oz ranch seasoning
- ½ cup of coconut milk
- ½ cup sour cream
- 10 oz cream of chicken soup
- 2 carrots, chopped
- 2 cups potatoes, diced
- 1 cup chicken stock
- 2 celery stalks, diced
- 1 onion, diced
- 1 tbsp olive oil
- Pepper
- Salt

Directions:

- Add oil into the instant pot and set the pot on sauté mode.

- Add celery and onion to the pot and sauté until onion is softened about 5 minutes.
- Add stock and stir well.
- Season chicken with pepper and salt and add it to the instant pot.
- Add carrots and potatoes and stir well.
- Seal pot with lid and cook on manual high pressure for 8 minutes.
- Release pressure using the quick release method than open the lid carefully.
- Remove chicken from pot and shred using a fork.
- Return shredded chicken to the pot.
- Set pot on sauté mode. Add green beans, coconut milk, ranch seasoning, sour cream, and cream of chicken soup to the pot and stir to combine.
- Cook stew on sauté mode for 5 minutes.
- Serve and enjoy.

Nutritional Value (Amount per Serving):

- Calories 469
- Fat 26.5 g
- Carbohydrates 26.7 g
- Sugar 5.4 g
- Protein 26.7 g
- Cholesterol 83 mg

7-Creamy Herb Chicken Stew

Preparation Time: 10 minutes

Cooking Time: 12 minutes

Serve: 6

Ingredients:

- 1 lb chicken breasts, skinless and boneless
- 3 cups chicken stock
- ½ tsp dried basil
- ½ tsp thyme
- 1 tsp ground sage
- 3 garlic cloves, minced
- 1 onion, diced
- 2 large celery stalks, cut into chunks
- 3 carrots, cut into chunks
- 2 potatoes, peeled and diced
- ¼ tsp black pepper
- 1 tsp kosher salt

Directions:

- Add all ingredients except chicken to the instant pot and stir well.
- Add chicken to the pot.

- Seal pot with lid and cook on manual high pressure for 12 minutes.
- Allow to release pressure naturally for 10 minutes then release using the quick release method.
- Remove chicken from pot and shred using a fork.
- Ladle out 2 cups of stew mixture from pot place into the bowl. Puree the stew mixture using an immersion blender until smooth.
- Return shredded chicken and blended stew mixture to the pot and stir well.
- Season with pepper and salt.
- Serve and enjoy.

Nutritional Value (Amount per Serving):

- Calories 224
- Fat 6 g
- Carbohydrates 17.5 g
- Sugar 3.8 g
- Protein 24.1 g
- Cholesterol 67 mg

8-Chicken Veggie Stew

Preparation Time: 10 minutes

Cooking Time: 40 minutes

Serve: 6

Ingredients:

- 3 lbs whole chicken
- 3 tbsp olive oil
- 1 tomato, chopped
- 1 onion, chopped
- 8 oz cauliflower, chopped
- 1 tbsp cayenne pepper
- 4 cups chicken stock
- 10 oz broccoli, chopped
- 1/2 tsp black pepper
- 2 tsp salt

Directions:

- Season chicken with pepper and salt. Set aside.
- Add oil into the instant pot and set the pot on sauté mode.
- Add onion to the pot and sauté for 3-5 minutes.
- Add tomato and sauté for 5 minutes.
- Add remaining ingredients and stir well.

- Seal pot with lid and cook on manual high pressure for 30 minutes.
- Allow to release pressure naturally then open the lid.
- Remove chicken from pot and shred using a fork.
- Ladle out 1 cup stew mixture from pot and place in a bowl. Puree the stew mixture using an immersion blender until smooth.
- Return shredded chicken to the pot along with blended stew mixture.
- Serve and enjoy.

Nutritional Value (Amount per Serving):

- Calories 535
- Fat 24.6 g
- Carbohydrates 8.4 g
- Sugar 3.3 g
- Protein 68.6 g
- Cholesterol 202 mg

9-Tasty Chicken Rice Soup

Preparation Time: 10 minutes

Cooking Time: 13 minutes

Serve: 6

Ingredients:

- 4 chicken thighs, skinless and boneless
- 1 tsp lemon zest
- 1/4 tbsp dried parsley
- 1/2 tsp thyme
- 1 tsp garlic powder
- 1 celery stalk, diced
- 1 onion, chopped
- 2 carrots, chopped
- 1 cup jasmine rice
- 2 tbsp fresh lemon juice
- 6 cups chicken stock
- Pepper
- Salt

Directions:

- Add all ingredients into the instant pot and stir well.
- Seal pot with lid and cook on high pressure for 8 minutes.

- Allow to release pressure naturally for 5 minutes then release using the quick release method.
- Remove chicken from pot and shred using a fork.
- Return shredded chicken to the pot and stir well.
- Serve and enjoy.

Nutritional Value (Amount per Serving):

- Calories 321
- Fat 7.9 g
- Carbohydrates 29.2 g
- Sugar 2.8 g
- Protein 31.4 g
- Cholesterol 87 mg

10-Healthy Coconut Chicken Soup

Preparation Time: 10 minutes

Cooking Time: 5 minutes

Serve: 6

Ingredients:

- 1 lb chicken thighs, boneless and cut into chunks
- 2 cups Swiss chard, chopped
- 10 oz can tomatoes
- 1 cup of coconut milk
- 1 oz ginger
- 5 garlic cloves
- 1 onion, chopped
- 2 celery stalks, chopped
- 1 tsp turmeric powder
- 1 tbsp chicken broth base

Directions:

- Add onion, half coconut milk, broth base, turmeric, tomatoes, ginger, and garlic into the food processor and process until smooth.
- Transfer blended mixture into the instant pot along with Swiss chard, celery, and chicken and stir well.
- Seal pot with lid and cook on high pressure for 5 minutes.

- Allow to release pressure naturally then open the lid.
- Add remaining coconut milk and stir well.
- Serve and enjoy.

Nutritional Value (Amount per Serving):

- Calories 311
- Fat 15.9 g
- Carbohydrates 19.1 g
- Sugar 2.9 g
- Protein 26.2 g
- Cholesterol 67 mg

MEAT SOUP & STEW

11-Delicious Beef Vegetable Soup

Preparation Time: 10 minutes

Cooking Time: 23 minutes

Serve: 8

Ingredients:

- 1 lb beef stew meat, cut into cubes
- 2 celery stalks, chopped
- 2 carrots, peeled and chopped
- 1 lb potatoes, peeled and cut into cube
- 2 cups of water
- 4 cups chicken broth
- ½ cup dry red wine
- 3 garlic cloves, minced
- ½ tsp thyme
- 1 tbsp tomato paste
- 1 onion, chopped

- 6 oz mushrooms, sliced
- 2 tbsp olive oil

Directions:

- Add 1 tablespoon of olive oil into the instant pot and set the pot on sauté mode.
- Add meat to the pot and sauté until meat is brown from all the side. Transfer meat in a bowl.
- Add remaining oil to the pot. Add onion and mushrooms and sauté for 5 minutes.
- Stir in garlic, thyme, and tomato paste and cook 30 seconds.
- Add broth, red wine, meat, celery, carrots, potatoes, and water. Stir well.
- Seal pot with lid and cook on soup mode for 17 minutes.
- Allow to release pressure naturally then open the lid.
- Stir and serve.

Nutritional Value (Amount per Serving):

- Calories 226
- Fat 7.9 g
- Carbohydrates 14.2 g
- Sugar 3.1 g
- Protein 21.7 g
- Cholesterol 51 mg

12-Hamburger Soup

Preparation Time: 10 minutes

Cooking Time: 20 minutes

Serve: 8

Ingredients:

- 1 lb ground beef
- ½ tbsp garlic, minced
- 3 cups chicken broth
- 14.5 oz can tomatoes, diced
- 1 cup of frozen green beans
- 1 ½ tbsp tomato paste
- 1 cup potatoes, diced
- 2 celery stalks, sliced
- 2 carrots, peeled and sliced
- 1 onion, chopped
- 2 tsp olive oil
- ½ tsp pepper
- 2 tsp sea salt

Directions:

- Add oil into the instant pot and set the pot on sauté mode.
- Add meat to the pot and cook until meat is browned.

- Add remaining ingredients and stir well to combine.
- Seal pot with lid and cook on manual high pressure for 15 minutes.
- Allow to release pressure naturally then open the lid.
- Stir well and serve.

Nutritional Value (Amount per Serving):

- Calories 174
- Fat 5.3 g
- Carbohydrates 10.6 g
- Sugar 4.2 g
- Protein 20.5 g
- Cholesterol 51 mg

Helena Walker

13-Flavorful Beef Barley Soup

Preparation Time: 10 minutes

Cooking Time: 13 minutes

Serve: 8

Ingredients:

- 1 lb beef stew meat, cut into cubes
- 6 oz mushrooms, quartered
- 3 garlic cloves, minced
- 1 ½ tsp Italian seasoning
- 1 onion, diced
- 2 celery stalks, chopped
- 2 carrots, peeled and chopped
- 4 cups chicken broth
- 14 oz can tomatoes, diced
- 1 cup dry pearl barley
- 1 tbsp olive oil
- ¼ tsp pepper
- ½ tsp salt

Directions:

- Add oil into the instant pot and set the pot on sauté mode.
- Add meat to the pot and season with pepper and salt.

- Sauté meat for 3-4 minutes or until lightly browned.
- Add mushrooms, Italian seasoning, garlic, onion, celery, and carrots and sauté for 2 minutes.
- Add barley, broth, and tomatoes and stir well.
- Seal pot with lid and cook on high pressure for 8 minutes.
- Allow to release pressure naturally then open the lid.
- Stir well and serve.

Nutritional Value (Amount per Serving):

- Calories 257
- Fat 6.3 g
- Carbohydrates 26.5 g
- Sugar 4 g
- Protein 26.5 g
- Cholesterol 51 mg

14-Beef Pasta Soup

Preparation Time: 10 minutes

Cooking Time: 20 minutes

Serve: 4

Ingredients:

- 1 lb lean ground beef
- 1 tbsp Italian seasoning
- 1 cup pasta, uncooked
- 14 oz can kidney beans, rinsed and drained
- 2 cups carrots, chopped
- 2 cups bell pepper, diced
- 2 celery stalks, chopped
- 1 cup tomato sauce
- 3 cups chicken stock
- 1 onion, diced
- 1 tbsp garlic, minced
- 2 tbsp olive oil
- ¼ tsp black pepper
- ½ tsp salt

Directions:

- Add oil into the instant pot and set the pot on sauté mode.

- Add onion and garlic to the pot and sauté for 2 minutes.
- Add meat and cook until meat is no longer pink. Stir constantly.
- Add stock and tomato sauce and stir well.
- Add bell peppers, carrots, celery, beans, and pasta. Stir well.
- Add seasonings and stir everything well.
- Seal pot with lid and cook on manual high pressure for 15 minutes.
- Allow to release pressure naturally for 10 minutes then release using the quick release method then open the lid.
- Stir well and serve.

Nutritional Value (Amount per Serving):

- Calories 538
- Fat 16.8 g
- Carbohydrates 54 g
- Sugar 12.3 g
- Protein 44.5 g
- Cholesterol 104 mg

15-Beef Cabbage Soup

Preparation Time: 10 minutes

Cooking Time: 10 minutes

Serve: 6

Ingredients:

- 1 lb ground beef
- 1 tsp garlic powder
- 1/4 tsp paprika
- 14 oz can tomatoes, diced
- ½ cabbage head, diced
- 5 cups chicken broth
- 2 tbsp olive oil
- ½ onion, sliced
- 2 garlic cloves, minced
- ¼ tsp pepper
- 1 tsp salt

Directions:

- Add olive oil into the instant pot and set the pot on sauté mode.
- Add ground beef, onion, and garlic to the pot and sauté until meat is browned.

- Add broth, garlic powder, paprika, tomatoes, and cabbage to the pot and stir well.
- Seal pot with lid and cook on manual high pressure for 5 minutes.
- Allow to release pressure naturally for 10 minutes then release pressure using the quick release method.
- Season soup with pepper and salt.
- Serve and enjoy.

Nutritional Value (Amount per Serving):

- Calories 249
- Fat 10.6 g
- Carbohydrates 9.2 g
- Sugar 5.3 g
- Protein 28.6 g
- Cholesterol 68 mg

16-Flavorful Beef Fajita Soup

Preparation Time: 10 minutes

Cooking Time: 25 minutes

Serve: 8

Ingredients:

- 1 lb beef stew meat, cut into cubes
- 1 ½ tsp ground cumin
- 1 onion, sliced
- 2 bell pepper, sliced
- 10 oz can tomatoes, diced
- 14 oz chicken broth
- 15 oz can black beans, rinsed and drained
- 15 oz can pinto beans, rinsed and drained
- ¼ tsp black pepper
- ½ tsp salt

Directions:

- Add all ingredients into the instant pot and stir well.
- Seal pot with lid and cook on manual high pressure for 25 minutes.
- Allow to release pressure naturally for 10 minutes then release using the quick release method.

- Stir well and serve.

Nutritional Value (Amount per Serving):

- Calories 232
- Fat 4.6 g
- Carbohydrates 23.3 g
- Sugar 4 g
- Protein 24.5 g
- Cholesterol 51 mg

17-Beef Lentil Stew

Preparation Time: 10 minutes

Cooking Time: 20 minutes

Serve: 4

Ingredients:

- 1 lb beef, cut into chunks
- 3 garlic cloves, minced
- 1 onion, diced
- 1 cup lentils, dry
- 1 1/2 tbsp curry powder
- 2 carrots, diced
- 3 potatoes, peeled and diced
- 28 oz can tomatoes, diced
- 4 cups chicken stock
- Pepper
- Salt

Directions:

- Add all ingredients in the instant pot and stir well.
- Seal pot with lid and cook on manual high pressure for 20 minutes.
- Allow releasing pressure naturally then open the lid.

- Stir well and serve.

Nutritional Value (Amount per Serving):

- Calories 577
- Fat 8.7 g
- Carbohydrates 72.5 g
- Sugar 13 g
- Protein 52.9 g
- Cholesterol 101 mg

18- Steak Mushroom Soup

Preparation Time: 10 minutes

Cooking Time: 15 minutes

Serve: 6

Ingredients:

- 1 lb steak, diced
- 1 large bell pepper, diced
- 2 large celery stalks, diced
- 2 large carrots, diced
- 2 cups of water
- 2 tbsp oregano
- 2 tbsp garlic powder
- 8 oz mushrooms, sliced
- 2 cups chicken stock
- 1 cup tomatoes, crushed
- 1 bay leaf
- 1 tbsp thyme
- 1 large onion, diced
- 1 tbsp salt

Directions:

- Set instant pot on sauté mode.

- Add meat to the pot and sauté until browned.
- Add onion, carrots, pepper, and celery and cook until softened.
- Add mushrooms and cook until softened.
- Add remaining ingredients into the pot and stir well.
- Seal pot with lid and cook on soup mode for 15 minutes.
- Release pressure using quick release method then open the lid.
- Stir and serve.

Nutritional Value (Amount per Serving):

- Calories 212
- Fat 4.4 g
- Carbohydrates 12 g
- Sugar 5.5 g
- Protein 31 g
- Cholesterol 68 mg

19-Simple Pork Cabbage Soup

Preparation Time: 10 minutes

Cooking Time: 30 minutes

Serve: 2

Ingredients:

- 1/2 lb ground pork
- 1 1/2 cup cabbage, chopped
- 1/2 tbsp soy sauce
- 2 cup beef stock
- 1 cup carrot, peeled and shredded
- 1 small onion, chopped
- 1/2 tsp ground ginger
- 1 tbsp olive oil
- Pepper
- Salt

Directions:

- Add oil into the instant pot and set the pot on sauté mode.
- Add meat to the pot and sauté for 3-4 minutes.
- Add remaining ingredients and stir well to combine.
- Seal pot with lid and cook on high pressure for 25 minutes.

- Release pressure using quick release method then open the lid.
- Season soup with pepper and salt.
- Serve and enjoy.

Nutritional Value (Amount per Serving):

- Calories 288
- Fat 11.7 g
- Carbohydrates 13.4 g
- Sugar 6.7 g
- Protein 32.4 g
- Cholesterol 83 mg

20-Lamb Stew

Preparation Time: 10 minutes

Cooking Time: 1 hour 25 minutes

Serve: 8

Ingredients:

- 4 lbs lamb shoulder, cut into chunks
- 4 cups beef stock
- 1 cup sour cream
- 1/2 lbs mushrooms, sliced
- 1 onion, diced
- 2 garlic cloves, minced
- 1 cup tomato puree
- 1/2 cup red wine vinegar
- 2 celery stalks, diced
- 3 tbsps rosemary, chopped
- 1/4 cup olive oil
- 1 tsp salt

Directions:

- Add oil into the instant pot and set the pot on sauté mode.
- Add celery, rosemary, onion, and garlic to the pot and sauté for 5 minutes.

- Add tomato puree, vinegar, pepper, and salt and cook for 5 minutes.
- Add stock and meat and stir well.
- Seal pot with lid and cook on meat/stew mode for 60 minutes.
- Allow to release pressure naturally then open the lid.
- Set instant pot on sauté mode.
- Add mushrooms and cook for 15 minutes more.
- Stir in sour cream and serve.

Nutritional Value (Amount per Serving):

- Calories 578
- Fat 29.6 g
- Carbohydrates 7.6 g
- Sugar 2.8 g
- Protein 67.7 g
- Cholesterol 217 mg

FISH & SEAFOOD SOUP & STEW

21-Tasty Fish Soup

Preparation Time: 10 minutes

Cooking Time: 13 minutes

Serve: 4

Ingredients:

- 1 lb halibut, skinless, boneless, and chopped
- 1 1/2 tbsp ginger, minced
- 2 celery stalks, chopped
- 1 carrot, sliced
- 1 onion, chopped
- 1 cup of water
- 2 cups beef stock
- 1 tbsp olive oil
- 2 tbsp fresh parsley, chopped
- Pepper
- Salt

Directions:

- Add oil into the instant pot and set the pot on sauté mode.
- Add onion to the pot and sauté for 3-4 minutes.
- Add water, celery, carrot, ginger, and stock and stir well.
- Seal pot with lid and cook on high for 5 minutes.
- Release pressure using the quick release method than open the lid.
- Add fish pieces to the pot and cook on manual low pressure for 4 minutes.
- Release pressure using the quick release method than open the lid carefully.
- Garnish soup with parsley and serve.

Nutritional Value (Amount per Serving):

- Calories 213
- Fat 6.6 g
- Carbohydrates 6 g
- Sugar 2.1 g
- Protein 33.2 g
- Cholesterol 47 mg

22-Flavorful Fish Stew

Preparation Time: 10 minutes

Cooking Time: 25 minutes

Serve: 6

Ingredients:

- 1 ½ lbs cod, skinless, boneless, and cut into pieces
- 1 tbsp fresh parsley, chopped
- 1 tbsp fresh lime juice
- 2 tbsp olive oil
- ¼ tsp cayenne
- ½ tbsp paprika
- ½ tbsp ground cumin
- 6 oz coconut oil
- 8 oz chicken broth
- 14 oz can tomatoes, crushed
- 4 garlic cloves, minced
- 1 bell pepper, sliced
- 1 onion, diced
- ¼ tsp black pepper
- ½ tsp salt

Directions:

- Add all ingredients except parsley, lime juice, and cod to the instant pot and stir well.
- Seal pot with lid and cook on manual high pressure for 10 minutes.
- Allow to release pressure naturally for 10 minutes then release using the quick release method.
- Set pot on sauté mode and cook the stew for 10 minutes or until thickened.
- Stir in fish and cook for 5 minutes or until fish is cooked.
- Turn off the instant pot. Stir in lime juice.
- Garnish with parsley and serve.

Nutritional Value (Amount per Serving):

- Calories 446
- Fat 34.5 g
- Carbohydrates 8.7 g
- Sugar 4.4 g
- Protein 28 g
- Cholesterol 62 mg

23-Seafood Stew

Preparation Time: 10 minutes

Cooking Time: 11 minutes

Serve: 6

Ingredients:

- 1 lb shrimp, cleaned and deveined
- 1 1/2 lbs fish, cut into chunks
- 1/4 cup cilantro, chopped
- 10 littleneck clams
- 1 cup chicken stock
- 2 garlic cloves, minced
- 1 1/2 cups tomatoes, diced
- 1 bell pepper, sliced
- 1 onion, sliced
- 1 1/2 tsp paprika
- 1 bay leaf
- 3 tbsp olive oil
- Sea salt

Directions:

- Add olive oil into the instant pot and set the pot on sauté mode.

- Add paprika and bay leaf and stir for 30 seconds.
- Add onion, cilantro, garlic, tomatoes, bell pepper, pepper, and salt. Stir well.
- Add water and fish stock.
- Add remaining ingredients to the pot and stir well.
- Seal pot with lid and cook on manual high pressure for 10 minutes.
- Allow releasing pressure naturally then open the lid.
- Stir well and serve.

Nutritional Value (Amount per Serving):

- Calories 457
- Fat 22.8 g
- Carbohydrates 26.7 g
- Sugar 3.2 g
- Protein 38 g
- Cholesterol 206 mg

24-Shrimp Soup

Preparation Time: 10 minutes

Cooking Time: 25 minutes

Serve: 6

Ingredients:

- 2 lbs shrimp
- ½ tsp dried rosemary
- 4 cups chicken stock
- 2 tbsps butter
- 2 tbsps olive oil
- ¼ cup fresh parsley, chopped
- 1 tomato, chopped
- 3 garlic cloves, minced
- 1 cup broccoli, cut into florets
- 1 ½ tsps sea salt

Directions:

- Add oil into the instant pot and set the pot on sauté mode.
- Add broccoli to the pot and sauté until lightly brown.
- Add garlic and sauté for a minute.
- Add tomatoes and cook for 5-7 minutes.
- Add shrimp, rosemary, and salt and stir well.

- Add remaining ingredients and stir everything well.
- Seal pot with lid and cook on manual high pressure for 15 minutes.
- Release pressure using the quick release method than open the lid.
- Serve hot and enjoy.

Nutritional Value (Amount per Serving):

- Calories 271
- Fat 11.6 g
- Carbohydrates 4.9 g
- Sugar 1 g
- Protein 35.6 g
- Cholesterol 329 mg

25-Fish Veggie Stew

Preparation Time: 10 minutes

Cooking Time: 8 minutes

Serve: 6

Ingredients:

- 1 lb cod fish fillets, cut into pieces
- 2 tbsp olive oil
- 1 cup kale, chopped
- 1 cup cauliflower, chopped
- 1 cup broccoli, chopped
- 3 cups chicken stock
- ½ cup heavy cream
- 2 celery stalks, diced
- 1 carrot, sliced
- 1 onion, diced
- Pepper
- Salt

Directions:

- Add oil into the instant pot and set the pot on sauté mode.
- Add onion to the pot and sauté for 3 minutes.
- Add remaining ingredients except for cream and stir well.

- Seal pot with lid and cook on manual high pressure for 5 minutes.
- Allow to release pressure naturally then open the lid.
- Stir in heavy cream and serve.

Nutritional Value (Amount per Serving):

- Calories 186
- Fat 9.4 g
- Carbohydrates 6.6 g
- Sugar 2.4 g
- Protein 19.2 g
- Cholesterol 55 mg

VEGETABLE SOUP & STEW

26-Basil Tomato Soup

Preparation Time: 10 minutes

Cooking Time: 35 minutes

Serve: 6

Ingredients:

- 28 oz can tomatoes
- 1/3 cup Romano cheese, grated
- 1 bay leaf
- 1/2 cup fresh basil, chopped
- 1 fresh thyme sprig
- 2 carrots, diced
- 1 3/4 cups coconut milk
- 3 1/2 cups chicken stock
- 1 cup onion, diced
- 1 cup celery, diced
- 1 tbsp butter

- 2 tbsps olive oil
- Pepper
- Salt

Directions:

- Add oil and butter into the instant pot and set the pot on sauté mode.
- Add celery, onion, and carrots and sauté for 5 minutes.
- Add remaining ingredients and stir well.
- Seal pot with lid and cook on manual high pressure for 30 minutes.
- Release pressure using quick release method then open the lid.
- Puree the soup using an immersion blender until smooth.
- Stir well and serve.

Nutritional Value (Amount per Serving):

- Calories 299
- Fat 25.6 g
- Carbohydrates 13 g
- Sugar 7 g
- Protein 7.8 g
- Cholesterol 10 mg

27-Delicious Squash Soup

Preparation Time: 10 minutes

Cooking Time: 8 minutes

Serve: 6

Ingredients:

- 6 cups butternut squash, peeled and cubed
- 3 cups vegetable stock
- 1 onion, chopped
- 2 tbsp butter
- 1/4 cup heavy cream
- 1/8 tsp nutmeg
- 1/2 tsp cayenne pepper
- 2 tsps thyme
- Pepper
- Salt

Directions:

- Add butter into the instant pot and set the pot on sauté mode.
- Add onion to the pot and sauté for 3 minutes.
- Add squash, nutmeg, cayenne, thyme, stock, and salt. Stir well.

- Seal pot with lid and cook on high for 5 minutes.
- Allow to release pressure naturally then open the lid.
- Stir in heavy cream. Puree the soup using an immersion blender until smooth.
- Season soup with pepper and salt
- Serve and enjoy.

Nutritional Value (Amount per Serving):

- Calories 88
- Fat 7 g
- Carbohydrates 8.1 g
- Sugar 1.8 g
- Protein 1.9 g
- Cholesterol 17 mg

28-Healthy Vegetable Stew

Preparation Time: 10 minutes

Cooking Time: 13 minutes

Serve: 4

Ingredients:

- 1 1/2 lbs potatoes, peeled and cut into 1-inch pieces
- 2 large carrots, peeled and sliced
- 1 tbsp flour
- 1 celery stalk, sliced
- 1 leek, sliced
- 1 tsp olive oil
- 2 cups vegetable stock
- 1/2 cup frozen peas
- 1/2 tsp Worcestershire sauce
- 1/2 cup mushroom, diced
- 1/2 tsp herb de Provence
- 1/4 tsp pepper
- 1/4 tsp salt

Directions:

- Add olive oil into the instant pot and set the pot on sauté mode.

- Add mushrooms and sauté for 2 minutes.
- Add celery, potatoes, carrots, Worcestershire sauce, herbs, vegetable stock, pepper, and salt. Stir well.
- Seal pot with lid and cook on stew mode for 10 minutes.
- Allow release of pressure naturally then open lid carefully.
- In a small bowl, whisk flour and 1 tablespoon of water.
- Add flour slurry and frozen peas to the pot and stir well.
- Cook stew on sauté mode for 1 minute.
- Serve and enjoy.

Nutritional Value (Amount per Serving):

- Calories 187
- Fat 2.1 g
- Carbohydrates 39.3 g
- Sugar 6.6 g
- Protein 5.4 g
- Cholesterol 0 mg

Helena Walker

29-Creamy Carrot Soup

Preparation Time: 10 minutes

Cooking Time: 10 minutes

Serve: 6

Ingredients:

- 8 carrots, peeled and cut into pieces
- 1/2 fresh lemon juice
- 2 tbsps butter
- 2 garlic cloves
- 1/2 onion, chopped
- 1/4 tsp ginger
- 1 1/2 tsps curry powder
- 4 cups vegetable stock
- 1 tsp salt

Directions:

- Add butter into the instant pot and set the pot on sauté mode.
- Add onion and garlic to the pot and sauté for 2 minutes.
- Add 1 cup stock, curry powder, and carrots. Stir well.
- Seal pot with lid and cook on manual high pressure for 8 minutes.

- Release pressure using quick release method than open the lid.
- Add remaining stock and using immersion blender puree the soup until smooth.
- Add lemon juice, ginger,s and salt and stir well.
- Serve and enjoy.

Nutritional Value (Amount per Serving):

- Calories 82
- Fat 5.3 g
- Carbohydrates 11 g
- Sugar 5.8 g
- Protein 1 g
- Cholesterol 10 mg

30-Mushroom Soup

Preparation Time: 10 minutes

Cooking Time: 11 minutes

Serve: 2

Ingredients:

- 1 cup mushrooms, chopped
- 1/4 tsp chili powder
- 5 cups chicken stock
- 2 fresh celery stalks, chopped
- 2 garlic cloves, crushed
- 1 onion, chopped
- 1 1/2 tsps garam masala
- 2 tbsps olive oil
- 1 tsp fresh lemon juice
- 1/2 tsp black pepper
- 1 tsp sea salt

Directions:

- Add oil into the instant pot and set the pot on sauté mode.
- Add garlic and onion and sauté for 5 minutes.
- Add chili powder and garam masala and cook for a minute.

- Add remaining ingredients and stir everything well.
- Seal pot with lid and cook on high pressure for 5 minutes.
- Release pressure using quick release method then open the lid
- Puree the soup using an immersion blender until smooth.
- Serve and enjoy.

Nutritional Value (Amount per Serving):

- Calories 188
- Fat 15.8 g
- Carbohydrates 10.9 g
- Sugar 5.3 g
- Protein 4 g
- Cholesterol 0 mg

MEXICAN SOUP & STEW

31-Black Bean Soup

Preparation Time: 10 minutes

Cooking Time: 5 minutes

Serve: 4

Ingredients:

- 4 cups can black beans
- 2 cups frozen corn
- 1 tsp chili powder
- 4 cups chicken stock
- 16 oz salsa
- 1 tsp cumin
- 1 tsp salt

Directions:

- Add all ingredients except corn into the instant pot and stir well.
- Seal pot with lid and cook on high pressure for 5 minutes.
- Allow to release pressure naturally for 15 minutes then release using the quick release method.
- Stir in corn and serve.

Nutritional Value (Amount per Serving):

- Calories 350
- Fat 2.9 g
- Carbohydrates 68.9 g
- Sugar 8.7 g
- Protein 19.1 g
- Cholesterol 0 mg

Helena Walker

32-Low- Carb Taco Soup

Preparation Time: 10 minutes

Cooking Time: 20 minutes

Serve: 8

Ingredients:

- 2 lbs ground beef
- 20 oz can tomatoes, diced
- 1 ½ tsps ground cumin
- 1 ½ tbsps chili powder
- 2 garlic cloves, minced
- ½ cup heavy cream
- 8 oz cream cheese
- 4 cups chicken stock
- 1 tbsp olive oil
- Pepper
- Salt

Directions:

- Add oil into the instant pot and set the pot on sauté mode.
- Add meat in the pot and sauté for 10 minutes.
- Add remaining ingredients except for heavy cream and cream cheese. Stir well.

- Seal pot with lid and cook on soup mode for 10 minutes.
- Allow to release pressure naturally then open the lid.
- Stir in heavy cream and cream cheese.
- Serve and enjoy.

Nutritional Value (Amount per Serving):

- Calories 394
- Fat 22.6 g
- Carbohydrates 6.7 g
- Sugar 3 g
- Protein 40.1 g
- Cholesterol 143 mg

33-Veggie Bean Soup

Preparation Time: 10 minutes

Cooking Time: 30 minutes

Serve: 6

Ingredients:

- 1 cup dried white beans
- 1 cup dried pinto beans
- 1 cup dried kidney beans
- 1 bell pepper, chopped
- 6 cups vegetable stock
- 3 garlic cloves, minced
- 1 onion, chopped
- 3 carrots, chopped
- 3 celery stalks, chopped
- 1 bay leaf
- Salt

Directions:

- Add all ingredients to the instant pot and stir well.
- Seal pot with lid and cook on soup mode for 30 minutes.
- Allow for the release of pressure naturally then open the lid.

- Stir well and serve.

Nutritional Value (Amount per Serving):

- Calories 367
- Fat 3.1 g
- Carbohydrates 68.2 g
- Sugar 7.4 g
- Protein 22.5 g
- Cholesterol 0 mg

Helena Walker

34-Flavorful Taco Soup

Preparation Time: 10 minutes

Cooking Time: 30 minutes

Serve: 6

Ingredients:

- 2 lbs ground beef
- 3 bell peppers, diced
- 1 large onion, diced
- 1 1/2 tbsps olive oil
- 8 oz green chilies, diced
- 5 oz coconut milk
- 24 oz chicken stock
- 28 oz tomatoes, diced
- 1/4 tsp cayenne pepper
- 1/2 tsp onion powder
- 1/2 tsp garlic powder
- 1 tsp cinnamon
- 1/2 tsp paprika
- 1 1/2 tsps black pepper
- 2 tbsps cumin
- 1 1/2 tbsps chili powder
- 2 tsps sea salt

Directions:

- Add oil into the instant pot and set the pot on sauté mode.
- Add bell peppers and onion to the pot and sauté for 5 minutes.
- Add ground beef and cook until meat is no longer pink.
- Add all spices and stir well.
- Add stock, green chilies, coconut milk, and tomatoes and stir well.
- Seal pot with lid and cook on soup mode for 25 minutes.
- Release pressure using quick release method than open the lid.
- Stir well and serve.

Nutritional Value (Amount per Serving):

- Calories 784
- Fat 25.2 g
- Carbohydrates 20.9 g
- Sugar 11 g
- Protein 114.5 g
- Cholesterol 100 mg

35-Chicken Tortilla Soup

Preparation Time: 10 minutes

Cooking Time: 20 minutes

Serve: 6

Ingredients:

- 1 1/2 lbs chicken breasts, skinless and boneless
- 20 oz can tomatoes
- 1 tsp cumin
- 1/2 tsp onion powder
- 2 tsps garlic powder
- 1 onion, chopped
- 2 chipotle peppers in adobo sauce
- 14 oz chicken stock
- 14 oz can coconut milk
- 1 tsp dried oregano
- 1 1/2 tsps chili powder
- 2 zucchinis, chopped
- 1 tsp paprika
- 1 1/2 tsps salt

Directions:

- Season chicken with salt and place in the instant pot.

- Add remaining ingredients except for coconut milk into the pot.
- Seal pot with lid and cook on high pressure for 20 minutes.
- Allow to release pressure naturally then open the lid.
- Remove chicken from pot and shred using a fork.
- Return shredded chicken to the pot along with coconut milk.
- Stir well and serve.

Nutritional Value (Amount per Serving):

- Calories 395
- Fat 23.1 g
- Carbohydrates 12.5 g
- Sugar 5.7 g
- Protein 36.6 g
- Cholesterol 101 mg

ASIAN SOUP & STEW

36-Perfect Thai Curry Soup

Preparation Time: 10 minutes

Cooking Time: 15 minutes

Serve: 4

Ingredients:

- ½ lb shrimp, peeled and deveined
- 1 cup baby spinach
- 14 oz coconut milk
- 14 oz chicken stock
- 2 ½ tbsps Thai red curry paste
- 1 sweet potato, peeled and chopped
- 3 tbsps olive oil
- 1 ½ tsps honey
- 3 tsps soy sauce
- ¼ tsp salt

Directions:

- In a mixing bowl, toss shrimp with 1 tsp honey and 1 tsp soy sauce until well coated and set aside.
- Add 1 tablespoon of oil in the instant pot and set the pot on sauté mode.
- Add shrimp to the pot and cook until shrimp turns pink. Remove shrimp from pot and place in a bowl.
- Add remaining oil to the pot. Add sweet potato and curry paste to the pot and sauté for 1-2 minutes.
- Add stock and stir well. Seal pot with lid and cook on soup mode for 5 minutes.
- Release pressure using the quick release method than open the lid carefully.
- Add spinach, coconut milk, shrimp, salt, remaining honey and soy sauce. Stir well.
- Set pot on sauté mode and cook for 2 minutes more.
- Stir well and serve.

Nutritional Value (Amount per Serving):

- Calories 465
- Fat 38.2 g
- Carbohydrates 17.2 g
- Sugar 7.7 g
- Protein 16.5g
- Cholesterol 119 mg

37-Beef Kimchi Stew

Preparation Time: 10 minutes

Cooking Time: 15 minutes

Serve: 6

Ingredients:

- 1 lb beef, cut into 2-inch cubes
- ¼ tsp sugar
- 1 tbsp red chili paste
- ½ tsp cayenne pepper
- 1/2 tbsp soy sauce
- 1 tbsp sesame oil
- 1 tbsp ginger, minced
- 1 tbsp garlic, minced
- 1 cup dried mushrooms
- 1 cup onion, chopped
- 2 cups of water
- 2 cups kimchi
- Salt

Directions:

- Add all ingredients into the instant pot and stir well.

- Seal pot with lid and cook on manual high pressure for 15 minutes.
- Release pressure using the quick release method than open the lid.
- Stir well and serve.

Nutritional Value (Amount per Serving):

- Calories 194
- Fat 7.7 g
- Carbohydrates 5.6 g
- Sugar 1.9 g
- Protein 24.6 g
- Cholesterol 68 mg

38-Squash Curried Soup

Preparation Time: 10 minutes

Cooking Time: 40 minutes

Serve: 4

Ingredients:

- 3 lbs butternut squash, peeled and cubed
- 1 tbsp curry powder
- 1/2 cup coconut milk
- 3 cups of water
- 2 garlic cloves, minced
- 1 onion, minced
- 1 tsp olive oil

Directions:

- Add olive oil into the instant pot and set the pot on sauté mode.
- Add onion to the pot and sauté for 8 minutes.
- Add curry powder and garlic and sauté for a minute.
- Add squash, water, and salt and stir well.
- Seal pot with lid and cook on soup mode for 30 minutes.
- Allow to release pressure naturally for 10 minutes then release using quick release method then open the lid.

- Puree the soup using an immersion blender until smooth.
- Stir in coconut milk and serve.

Nutritional Value (Amount per Serving):

- Calories 250
- Fat 8.9 g
- Carbohydrates 45.4 g
- Sugar 9.7 g
- Protein 4.7 g
- Cholesterol 0 mg

39-Indian Tomato Soup

Preparation Time: 10 minutes

Cooking Time: 5 minutes

Serve: 4

Ingredients:

- 6 Roma tomatoes, chopped
- 1 tsp garlic, minced
- 1/4 cup fresh parsley, chopped
- 1 onion, diced
- 14 oz coconut milk
- 1 tsp turmeric
- 1/2 tsp cayenne pepper
- 1 tsp ginger, minced
- 1 tsp salt

Directions:

- Add all ingredients to the instant pot and stir well.
- Seal instant pot with lid and cook on manual high pressure for 5 minutes.
- Allow to release pressure naturally for 10 minutes then release using the quick release method.
- Puree the soup using an immersion blender until smooth and creamy.

- Stir well and serve.

Nutritional Value (Amount per Serving):

- Calories 263
- Fat 8.2 g
- Carbohydrates 11 g
- Sugar 4.6 g
- Protein 36.7 g
- Cholesterol 101 mg

40-Coconut Cauliflower Soup

Preparation Time: 10 minutes

Cooking Time: 15 minutes

Serve: 4

Ingredients:

- 2 cups cauliflower florets
- 1/8 tsp thyme
- 1 1/3 tbsps curry powder
- 2/3 cups carrots, diced
- 1 cup onion, diced
- 1 1/3 tbsps olive oil
- 2/3 cups cashews, chopped
- 8 oz can coconut milk
- 2 2/3 cups vegetable broth
- 1/8 tsp black pepper
- 1/8 tsp salt

Directions:

- Add oil into the instant pot and set the pot on sauté mode.
- Add carrots, onion, and cauliflower to the pot and sauté for 5 minutes.

- Add remaining ingredients except for coconut milk and cashews and stir well.
- Seal instant pot with lid and cook on manual high pressure for 10 minutes.
- Allow to release pressure naturally then open the lid.
- Add coconut milk and stir well.
- Puree the soup using an immersion blender until smooth and creamy.
- Garnish with cashews and serve.

Nutritional Value (Amount per Serving):

- Calories 263
- Fat 8.2 g
- Carbohydrates 11 g
- Sugar 4.6 g
- Protein 36.7 g
- Cholesterol 101 mg

41-Kale Lentil Soup

Preparation Time: 10 minutes

Cooking Time: 15 minutes

Serve: 4

Ingredients:

- 2 1/2 cups kale leaves, chopped
- 2 cups of water
- 3 cups vegetable stock
- 3 whole cloves
- 2 cinnamon sticks
- 2 bay leaves
- 1 tbsp ginger, grated
- 2 garlic cloves, minced
- 1 tsp cumin powder
- 1 1/2 cups green lentils, rinsed
- 1 onion, chopped
- 1/2 tsp turmeric
- 1/2 tsp black pepper
- 1 tsp chili powder
- 3 tomatoes, chopped
- 2 carrots, peeled and chopped
- 1 tbsp vegetable oil
- Salt

Directions:

- Add oil into the instant pot and set the pot on sauté mode.
- Add cloves, cinnamon, and bay leave into the hot oil and sauté for a minute.
- Add garlic and ginger and sauté for a minute.
- Add onion and sauté for 1 minute.
- Add kale and cook for 30 seconds.
- Add tomatoes, carrots, and all spices and stir for a minute.
- Add lentils, salt, water, and stock and stir for 30 seconds.
- Seal pot with lid and cook on high pressure for 10 minutes.
- Release pressure using quick release method then open the lid.
- Stir well and serve.

Nutritional Value (Amount per Serving):

- Calories 263
- Fat 8.2 g
- Carbohydrates 11 g
- Sugar 4.6 g
- Protein 36.7 g
- Cholesterol 101 mg

42-Creamy Carrot Lentil Soup

Preparation Time: 10 minutes

Cooking Time: 16 minutes

Serve: 4

Ingredients:

- 3/4 cup red lentils, rinsed
- 4 carrots, peeled and chopped
- 1 1/2 tbsps curry powder
- 1 tbsp ginger, grated
- 1/2 onion, diced
- 1/4 tsp black pepper
- 4 cups vegetable stock
- 2 tsps vegetable oil
- 1 tsp kosher salt

Directions:

- Add oil into the instant pot and set the pot on sauté mode.
- Add onion to the pot and sauté for 5 minutes.
- Add curry powder and ginger and sauté for 30 seconds.
- Add lentils, stock, carrots, pepper, and salt and stir well to combine.

- Seal pot with lid and cook on manual high pressure for 10 minutes.
- Allow to release pressure naturally for 10 minutes then release using the quick release method.
- Puree the soup using an immersion blender until smooth.
- Serve and enjoy.

Nutritional Value (Amount per Serving):

- Calories 263
- Fat 8.2 g
- Carbohydrates 11 g
- Sugar 4.6 g
- Protein 36.7 g
- Cholesterol 101 mg

43-Lentil Squash Soup

Preparation Time: 10 minutes

Cooking Time: 17 minutes

Serve: 6

Ingredients:

- 1 1/2 cups red lentils, rinsed
- 1 lb butternut squash, cubed
- 2 whole cardamom pods, cracked
- 1-star anise
- 14 oz can tomato sauce
- 8 cups vegetable stock
- 1/4 tsp ground white pepper
- 2 tbsps curry powder
- 1 onion, diced
- 2 tbsps vegetable oil
- 2 tsps kosher salt

Directions:

- Add oil into the instant pot and set the pot on sauté mode.
- Add onion to the pot and sauté for 5 minutes.
- Add cardamom, star anise, white pepper, curry powder, and salt. Stir well.

- Add tomato sauce, stock, and butternut squash and stir well.
- Add lentils and stir well.
- Seal pot with lid and cook on manual high pressure for 12 minutes.
- Allow to release pressure naturally then open the lid.
- Stir well and serve.

Nutritional Value (Amount per Serving):

- Calories 263
- Fat 8.2 g
- Carbohydrates 11 g
- Sugar 4.6 g
- Protein 36.7 g
- Cholesterol 101 mg

44-Tasty Yellow Lentil Soup

Preparation Time: 10 minutes

Cooking Time: 8 minutes

Serve: 4

Ingredients:

- 1 cup split yellow lentils, rinsed
- 3 garlic cloves, diced
- 1/2 tomato, diced
- 1/2 onion, diced
- 1 tsp cumin seeds
- 1/2 tsp chili powder
- 1/4 tsp turmeric
- 1 tbsp vegetable oil
- 3 cups of water
- 1 tsp salt

Directions:

- Add oil into the instant pot and set the pot on sauté mode.
- Add cumin seeds to the pot and let them crackle.
- Add garlic and onion and sauté for 2 minutes.
- Add chili powder, turmeric, tomatoes, and salt and sauté for 2 minutes.

- Add lentils and water and stir well.
- Seal pot with lid and cook on manual high pressure for 4 minutes.
- Allow to release pressure naturally for 5 minutes then release using the quick release method.
- Stir well and serve.

Nutritional Value (Amount per Serving):

- Calories 263
- Fat 8.2 g
- Carbohydrates 11 g
- Sugar 4.6 g
- Protein 36.7 g
- Cholesterol 101 mg

45-Asian Chicken Noodle Soup

Preparation Time: 10 minutes

Cooking Time: 9 minutes

Serve: 6

Ingredients:

- 2 cups chicken breast, cooked and chopped
- 1/2 tsp red pepper flakes
- 1 tbsp lime juice
- 1 tbsp honey
- 3 tbsps soy sauce
- 2 tbsps rice vinegar
- 2 tbsps ginger, grated
- 8 cups chicken stock
- 2 carrots, peeled and chopped
- 1 red bell pepper, chopped
- 8 oz spaghetti noodles, cut in half
- 1/4 cup green onion, chopped
- 1 tbsp sesame oil
- 2 garlic cloves, minced
- 1 onion, chopped
- 1/2 tbsp olive oil

Directions:

- Add oil into the instant pot and set the pot on sauté mode.
- Add peppers, onion, and carrots to the pot and sauté for 5 minutes.
- Add garlic, red pepper flakes, Lime juice, honey, soy sauce, vinegar, ginger, broth, spaghetti, and chicken. Stir well.
- Seal pot with lid and cook on soup mode for 4 minutes.
- Release pressure using quick release method than open the lid.
- Stir in green onions and sesame oil.
- Serve and enjoy.

Nutritional Value (Amount per Serving):

- Calories 239
- Fat 6 g
- Carbohydrates 33 g
- Sugar 7 g
- Protein 13.4 g
- Cholesterol 46 mg

EUROPEAN SOUP & STEW

46-Chickpea Chicken Soup

Preparation Time: 10 minutes

Cooking Time: 30 minutes

Serve: 4

Ingredients:

- 2 chicken breasts, boneless and skinless
- 15 oz can chickpeas, drained and rinsed
- 7 cups spinach
- 1 tsp garlic powder
- 1/4 tsp cinnamon
- 2 celery stalks, diced
- 1 onion, diced
- 8 cups chicken stock
- 1/4 cup fresh lemon juice
- 2 carrots, diced
- 1/2 tsp pepper

- 1/2 tsp sea salt

Directions:

- Add carrots, chickpeas, celery, and onions to the instant pot.
- Add chicken, stock, lemon juice, garlic powder, cinnamon, pepper, and salt.
- Seal pot with lid and cook on soup mode.
- Allow to release pressure naturally then open the lid.
- Remove chicken from pot and shred using a fork.
- Return shredded chicken to the pot along with spinach and stir for 1-2 minutes.
- Serve and enjoy.

Nutritional Value (Amount per Serving):

- Calories 263
- Fat 8.2 g
- Carbohydrates 11 g
- Sugar 4.6 g
- Protein 36.7 g
- Cholesterol 101 mg

Helena Walker

47-Chicken Mushroom Soup

Preparation Time: 10 minutes

Cooking Time: 15 minutes

Serve: 4

Ingredients:

- 1 lb chicken breast, cut into chunks
- 2 cups mushrooms, sliced
- 3 garlic cloves, minced
- 1 onion, sliced
- 1 tsp Italian seasoning
- 2 1/2 cups chicken stock
- 1 yellow squash, chopped
- 1 tsp black pepper
- 1 tsp salt

Directions:

- Add all ingredients into the instant pot and stir well.
- Seal pot with lid and cook on high pressure for 15 minutes.
- Allow to release pressure naturally for 10 minutes then release using the quick release method.
- Remove chicken from pot and puree the vegetable mixture using an immersion blender.

- Shred the chicken using a fork.
- Return shredded chicken to the pot and stir well.
- Serve and enjoy.

Nutritional Value (Amount per Serving):

- Calories 263
- Fat 8.2 g
- Carbohydrates 11 g
- Sugar 4.6 g
- Protein 36.7 g
- Cholesterol 101 mg

48-Cabbage Leek Soup

Preparation Time: 10 minutes

Cooking Time: 20 minutes

Serve: 4

Ingredients:

- 1/2 cabbage head, chopped
- 2 garlic cloves, minced
- 1 bell pepper, diced
- 3 celery ribs, diced
- 2 carrots, diced
- 1 tsp Creole seasoning
- 1 tsp Italian seasoning
- 4 cups chicken stock
- 2 tbsp olive oil
- 2 leeks, chopped
- 2 cups mixed salad greens
- Pepper
- Salt

Directions:

- Add oil into the instant pot and set the pot on sauté mode.

- Add all ingredients except salad greens into the pot and stir well.
- Seal pot with lid and cook on soup mode for 20 minutes.
- Release pressure using quick release method than open the lid.
- Add salad greens and stir until it wilts.
- Serve and enjoy.

Nutritional Value (Amount per Serving):

- Calories 263
- Fat 8.2 g
- Carbohydrates 11 g
- Sugar 4.6 g
- Protein 36.7 g
- Cholesterol 101 mg

49-Minestrone Soup

Preparation Time: 10 minutes

Cooking Time: 10 minutes

Serve: 4

Ingredients:

- 1/2 cup fresh spinach
- 4 cups vegetable stock
- 2 cups cooked cannellini beans
- 1 tsp basil, dried
- 28 oz tomatoes, chopped
- 1 cup dry pasta
- 1 tsp oregano
- 2 garlic cloves, minced
- 1 carrot, diced
- 1 onion, diced
- 2 celery stalks, diced
- 2 tbsps olive oil
- 1 bay leaf
- Pepper
- Salt

Directions:

- Add olive oil into the instant pot and set the pot on sauté mode.
- Add onion, garlic, celery, and carrot and cook until softened.
- Add pepper, oregano, and basil. Stir well.
- Add tomatoes, pasta, bay leaf, spinach, and stock. Stir well.
- Seal pot with lid and cook on high pressure for 6 minutes.
- Release pressure using the quick release method thesn open lid carefully.
- Add cooked cannellini beans and stir well.
- Serve and enjoy.

Nutritional Value (Amount per Serving):

- Calories 263
- Fat 8.2 g
- Carbohydrates 11 g
- Sugar 4.6 g
- Protein 36.7 g
- Cholesterol 101 mg

50-Hearty Italian Chicken Soup

Preparation Time: 10 minutes

Cooking Time: 40 minutes

Serve: 8

Ingredients:

- 1 lb chicken breasts, boneless
- 16 oz rotini pasta
- 8 cups chicken stock
- 1 bay leaf
- ½ tsp garlic salt
- 2 tbsps Italian seasoning
- 1 bell pepper, chopped
- 10 oz can tomatoes, diced
- 1 medium onion, chopped
- ½ tsp black pepper
- 2 carrots, diced
- Salt

Directions:

- Add all ingredients except pasta into the instant pot and stir well.

- Seal pot with lid and cook on high pressure for 30 minutes.
- Release pressure using the quick release method then open the lid,
- Remove chicken from pot and shred using a fork.
- Return shredded chicken to the pot and stir well.
- Set pot on sauté mode. Add pasta to the pot and cook for 8-10 minutes.
- Stir well and serve.

Nutritional Value (Amount per Serving):

- Calories 317
- Fat 7.2 g
- Carbohydrates 38.1 g
- Sugar 4.3 g
- Protein 24.3 g
- Cholesterol 94 mg

CONCLUSION

In this instant pot soup & stew cookbook, you will find a huge collection of healthy, delicious and nutritious soup & stew recipes. This book will help people to live a healthier lifestyle. All the recipes are made in instant pot. An instant pot makes soup healthier and its nutrition preserve technology fills your meals with essential nutrients intact including vitamins, minerals, and protein.

Thank you for buying this book! I really do hope you found the recipes as delicious and mouth-watering as I did.

Happy Cooking!

Made in the USA
Monee, IL
20 January 2025

10367189R00066